D1085417

LET'S INVESTIGATE
Shapes

LET'S INVESTIGATE
Shapes

By Marion Smoothey

Illustrated by Ted Evans

MARSHALL CAVENDISH
NEW YORK · LONDON · TORONTO · SYDNEY

Library Edition Published 1993

© Marshall Cavendish Corporation 1993

Published by Marshall Cavendish Corporation
2415 Jerusalem Avenue
PO Box 587
North Bellmore
New York 11710

Series created by Graham Beehag Book Design

Library of Congress Cataloging-in-Publication Data

Smoothey, Marion, 1943-
    Shapes / by Marion Smoothey; illustrated by Ted Evans.
       p. cm.. -- (Let's Investigate)
    Includes index.
    Summary: Explores the world of shapes and how they can be drawn, measured, and used in various activities.
    ISBN 1-85435-464-7 ISBN 1-85435-463-9 (set)
    1. Geometry -- Juvenile literature. [1. Shape. 2. Geometry.]
    I. Evans, Ted ill. II. Title. III. Series:
    Smoothey, Marion, 1943- Let's Investigate.
    QA445.5.566 1993   92-38224
    516---dc20   CIP
                                            AC

Printed in Singapore by Times Offset PTE Ltd
Bound in the United States

Contents

THINGS YOU WILL NEED

This book has many ideas for activities and things to make. You will need plenty of scrap paper, a sharp pencil, a ruler and a protractor for most of them.

Some of them also require colored pencils or felt-tip pens, a compass, scissors, paper glue and thin cardboard. For page 14 you need a piece of thin string.

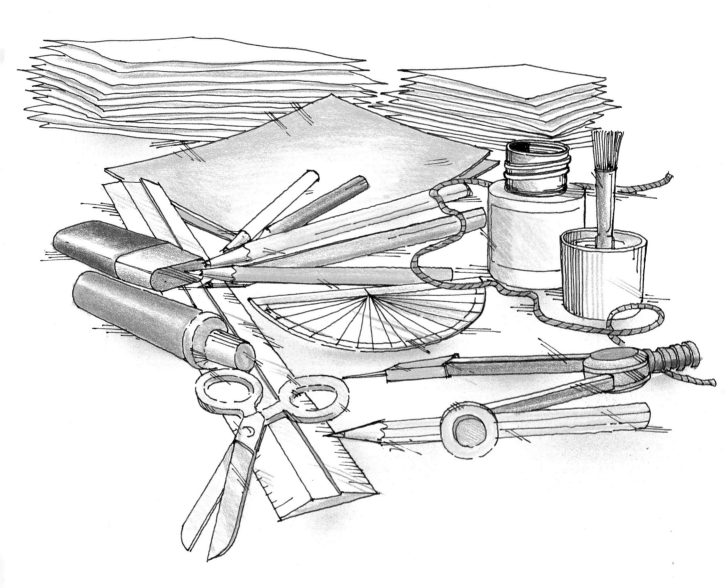

Shapes in the Everyday World

Look around the room or out of the window. You are surrounded by shapes. Some are made of straight lines, some from curves and some from a mixture of each.

7

The objects in our world are three-dimensional; they have length, width and depth. Mathematically we call them solids, even though they may be hollow – like an empty box or a tube. In mathematics, when we talk about shapes we mean two-dimensional objects which we represent by drawings on a page. When artists use perspective in their drawings, they are trying to make shapes look like solids.

If you look at the objects around you, you can see that their outlines make shapes. A ball is a **sphere**, but its outline is a circle. A ball is unusual because the shape of its outline is the same whichever way you look at it. If you look straight down on a can, its outline is a circle; if you look at it from the front, its outline is a rectangle.

8

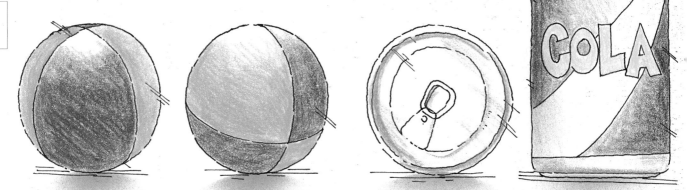

● How would an artist draw the top of a can in perspective?

These are the outlines of some common objects. There are two shapes for each object. Can you identify the objects?

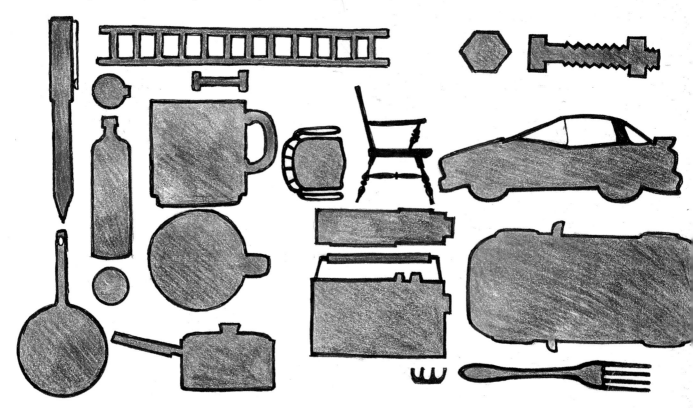

Doodles

On paper, make some doodles with a pencil. Color in the parts that are totally enclosed by lines. Go over in ink the lines that do not join up to enclose a colored shape.

The colored parts are **closed** shapes.
● Which of these are closed shapes?

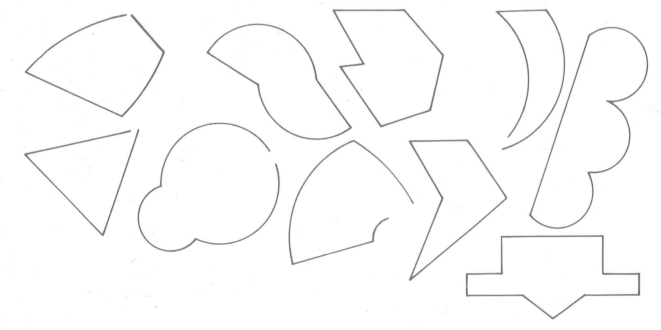

A Circle in Perspective

On a piece of thin cardboard, draw a circle. Mark the ends of a **diameter** on the **circumference**. Carefully cut around the circumference, except at the two marks.

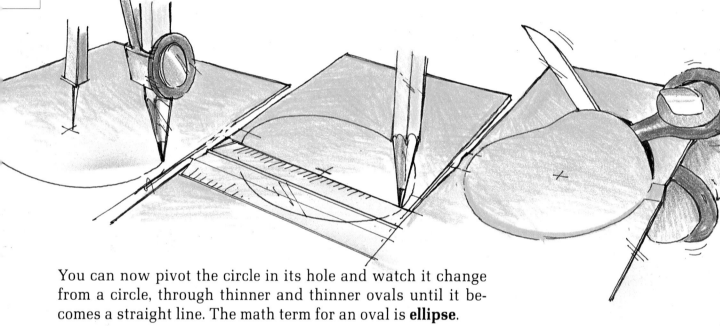

You can now pivot the circle in its hole and watch it change from a circle, through thinner and thinner ovals until it becomes a straight line. The math term for an oval is **ellipse**.

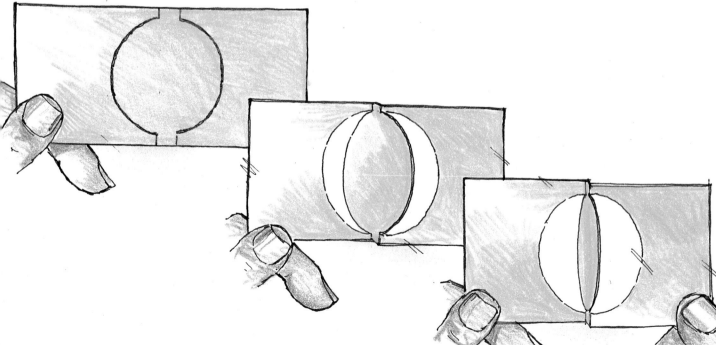

You can see the same thing by turning a plate held directly under a light source. Or shine a flashlight at a wall and change the angle at which you hold the flashlight.

You can see ellipses appear by viewing the top of a can from different angles. The artist used ellipses to draw the top of the can in perspective.

Side   Top

Shapes from Circles

You need a compass, a pencil and a ruler.

1. Mark two points **A** and **B** 2 inches apart. Set your compass to $\frac{1}{4}$". Draw a circle of $\frac{1}{4}$" radius with **A** as its center. Repeat for **B**.

This is quite difficult to do. Remember to adjust your pencil so that it touches the paper with the compass held upright. Hold your compass by the top, not the arms.

2. Set the compass to $\frac{1}{2}$". Draw two more circles with **A** and **B** as centers.

3. Continue to draw two sets of **concentric** circles at $\frac{1}{4}$" intervals with **A** and **B** as the centers, until you have drawn 2 sets of nine circles.

4. Number each set of circles from 1 to 9, starting with the smallest. Put a dot where circle **A1** touches circle **B9**. Put two dots where circle **A2** **intersects** with circle **B8**. Mark the intersection of circles **A3** and **B7** with dots. Continue in this pattern until you reach **A9** and **B1**.

5. Join the dots to form a shape.

● What is this shape called?

12

1.

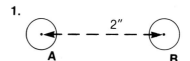

2.

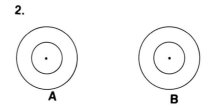

3.

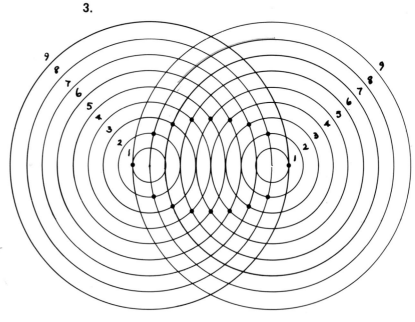

Shapes from Straight Lines

13

This shape is called an astroid.

You can draw it with a ruler and pencil. Draw two equal lines which **bisect** each other at **right angles** to form a cross. Mark off each arm of the cross in equal segments $-\frac{1}{4}$ " is a good size. Join the first mark on one arm to the last mark on an adjacent arm, the second mark on one arm to the second last mark on the adjacent arm and so on. Repeat for each side of each arm.

You can experiment with different arrangements and numbers of lines and see what shapes you get. If you find one you especially like, you can stitch it on cardboard with thread, like the example shown here.

Spirals

You can see spirals in the shape of a snail's shell, or in water as it swirls down the drain. The optical illusion they produce when spun around is sometimes used to attract attention to side-shows at fairs.

There are several ways to draw a spiral. Here is one of them. You may need a friend to help you.

You need about a foot of thin string, a pencil with a sharp point, another pencil and a piece of cardboard about 6 inches square.

Tie a small loop in one end of the string. Wind the string around one of the pencils until the loop is as close to the point as you can get it. Continue winding the string about half way up the pencil so that it is covered with one layer of string.

Attach one pencil to the cardboard with plastacine, and slip the other pencil point through the loop of string. Draw the spiral by unrolling the string from the pencil in the center with the other pencil. As long as you keep the string tight and the pencils upright, you can stop and start without spoiling the pattern.

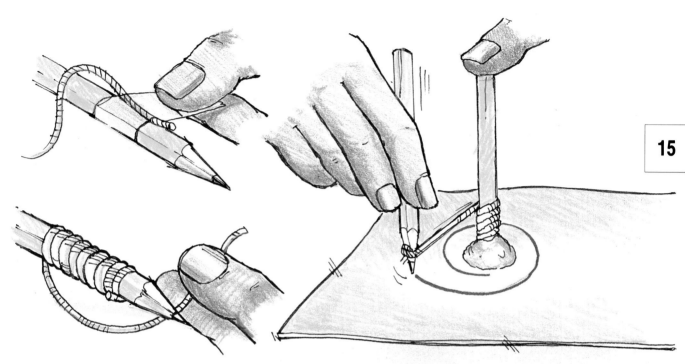

When you have filled the cardboard or run out of string, remove the pencil. Push the point of the pencil through from underneath and balance the cardboard on it.

If you spin the cardboard the spiral will appear to move inward or outward depending on which way around you spin it.

Sprouts

You need two or more players, each with a different colored pencil, and a piece of plain paper.

16

Draw five dots anywhere on the paper.

Each player, in turn, joins one dot to another with a line and marks another dot anywhere on the line. The line joining the dots does not have to be straight; it can twist and loop as much as you like. Each new dot on a line becomes part of the game and can be used by the other players.

There are two rules about the lines you can draw.
1. No line is allowed to cross another line.
2. There must be no more than three lines joined to each dot.

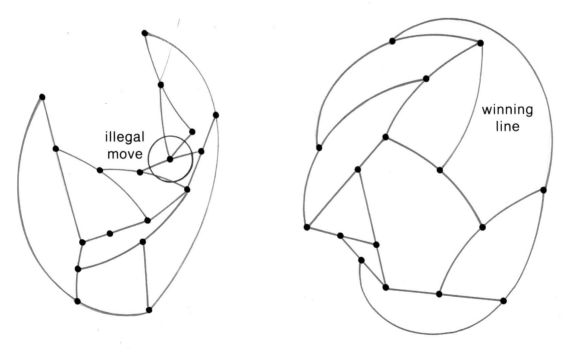

The winner is the player who draws the last line.

Polygons

These are polygons.

These are not polygons.

● Can you see what two things every polygon has in common?

The two things that every polygon has in common are:
1. A polygon must have straight sides.
2. The sides must join up with no gaps between them.

A polygon is a closed shape with straight sides.

Draw some polygons. Use a ruler and pencil.

18

● **1.** Draw a polygon with as few sides as you can. What is the name of this shape?

● **2.** Draw a convex polygon with a many sides as you can. What sort of shape does it begin to look like?

● **3.** Draw a star-shaped polygon.

● **4.** Draw six other polygons.

Keep your drawings. You will need them later.

Puzzle

Draw five dots on a piece of paper so that no three dots are in a straight line. How many ways are there of joining pairs of dots?

● If you draw all the ways on one diagram, what polygons do you get?

Names of Polygons

Number of Sides	Name
3	Triangle
4	Quadrilateral
5	Pentagon
6	Hexagon
7	Heptagon
8	Octagon
9	Nonagon
10	Decagon
12	Dodecagon

Some polygons have special names, according to how many sides they have.

● Copy the grid below and fit the names for these polygons into it. Do not write in the book.

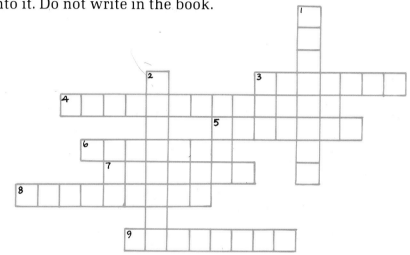

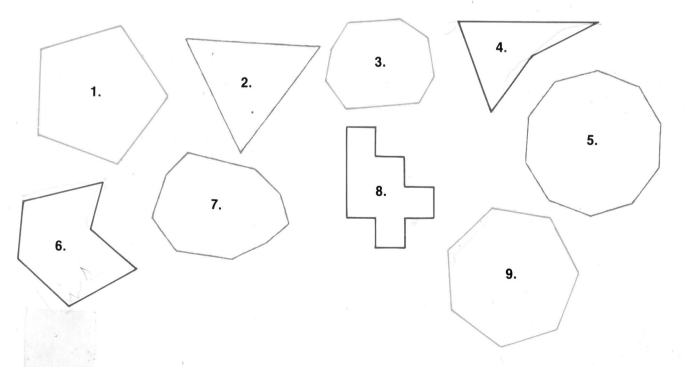

Making Polygons

Copy these shapes exactly onto thin cardboard and cut them out.

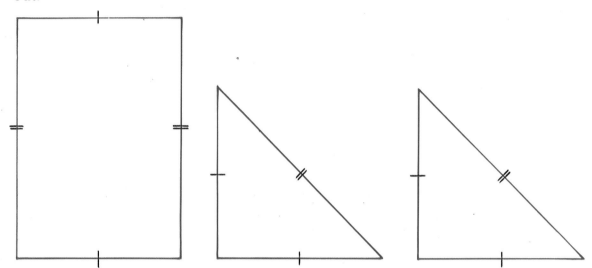

● Make as many different polygons as you can by matching equal sides together. Use all three pieces each time. Draw each one and name it. Here is one to get you started.

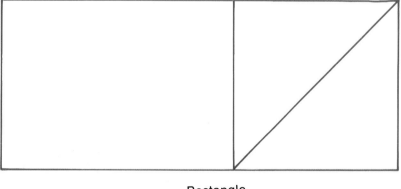

Rectangle

Answers to five dots puzzle

You can draw ten different lines.

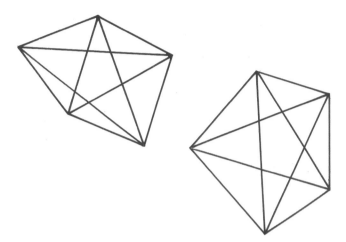

If you draw all the ways in one diagram, you can pick out two five-sided closed shapes (pentagons), a five-pointed star (a pentagram or pentangle), five quadrilaterals and many different triangles.

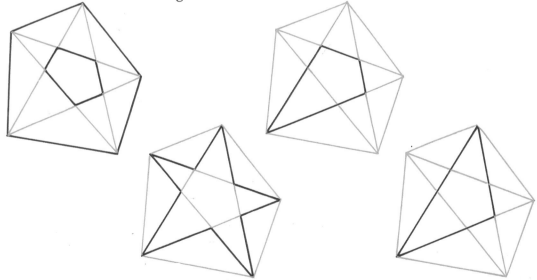

● How many triangles can you find?

Convex Polygons

On the edges of each of the polygons that you drew for page 18, mark two points **A** and **B**. Join **A** to **B**. Notice whether or not all of the line **AB** is inside the polygon.

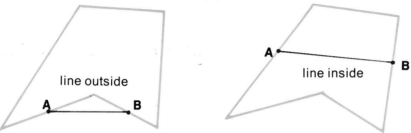

If it is not possible to draw a line **AB** so that part of it lies outside the polygon, the polygon is **convex**.

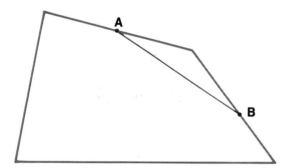

If it is possible to draw a line **AB** so that part of it lies outside the polygon, the polygon is not convex.

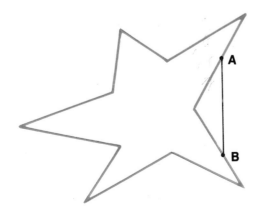

● Which of these polygons are convex?

● Can you draw a triangle that is not convex?

You can make these polygons from the shapes on page 20.

24

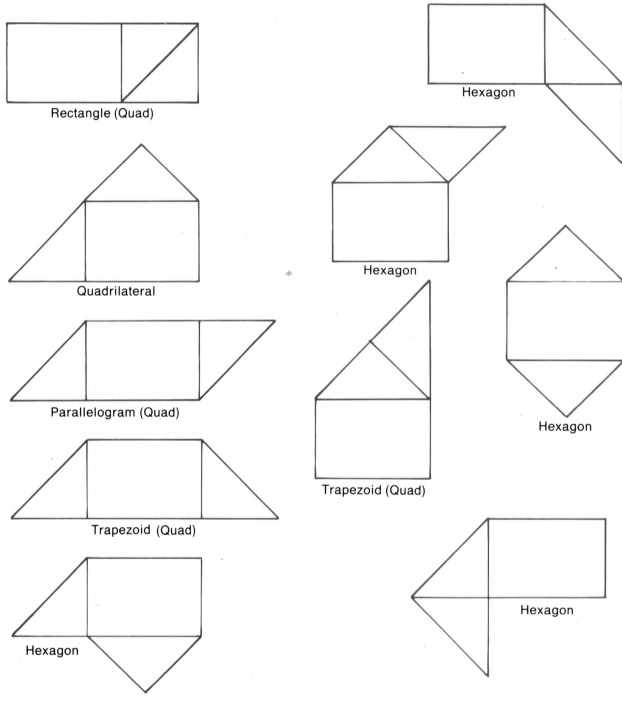

Rectangle (Quad)

Hexagon

Quadrilateral

Hexagon

Parallelogram (Quad)

Trapezoid (Quad)

Hexagon

Trapezoid (Quad)

Hexagon

Hexagon

Notice that they are all either hexagons or quadrilaterals. Some quadrilaterals have special names. A **parallelogram** has two pairs of parallel sides. A **trapezoid** only has one pair of parallel sides.

Regular Polygons

● Measure the sides of these polygons with a ruler. Measure their angles with a protractor. What do you notice?

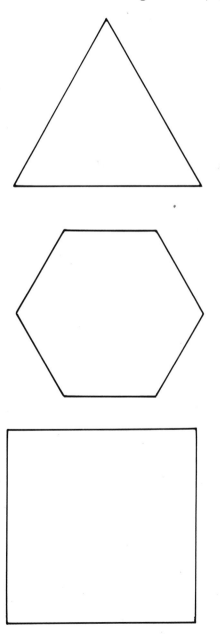

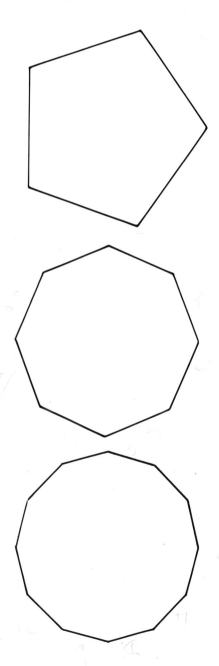

You should have found that in each polygon, the sides were of equal length, and the angles were of equal size.

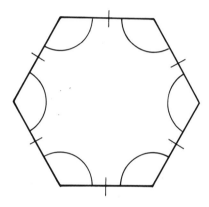

> A polygon in which all the sides are equal *and* all the angles are equal is called a **regular polygon**.

● Why is this hexagon not regular?

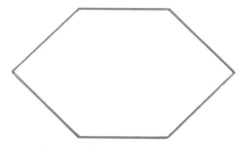

Answers to the polygon grid

Dots and Polygons

You need two or three sheets of graph paper.

1. Use the corners of the squares to mark out a grid of nine dots. Join any of the dots to make a polygon. Here is one way of joining some of the dots to make a triangle.

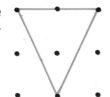

● Is this one polygon or two?

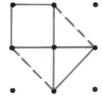

You could think of it as a pentagon with two of its sides reversed

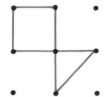

or as a triangle and a square touching each other.

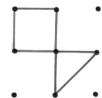

For these investigations, it is best to use ordinary polygons that don't have any lines crossing over each other.

● **2.** Try to make a polygon with the greatest number of sides possible in the grid of nine dots. What is the polygon's name?

● **3.** What is the greatest number of sides you can draw on a grid of sixteen dots?

● **4.** What is the greatest number of sides you can draw on a grid of twenty-five dots?

Answer to page 26

The hexagon was not regular because its angles were not all the same size.

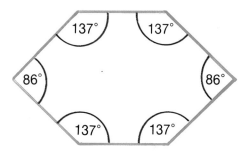

- Which of these are the regular polygons?

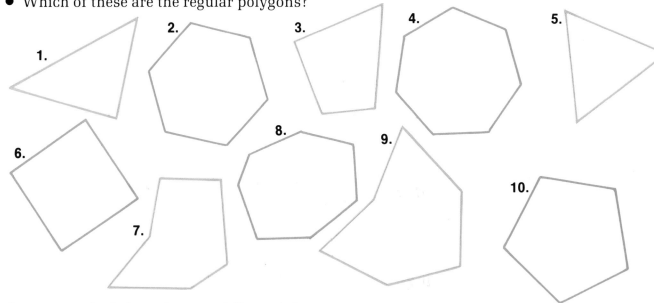

Answers to triangles and five dots

There are 35 triangles.

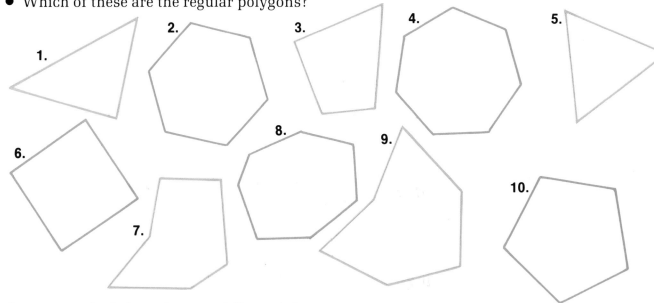

| There are 10 small triangles. | 1 × 5 Each diagonal has a triangle similar to this. | 2 × 5 Each diagonal has two overlapping triangles. | 1 × 5 There is a large triangle on each side of the pentagon. | 1 × 5 Each diagonal has a triangle similar to this. |

Answers to dots and polygons

The polygon with the greatest number of sides that you can draw on a grid of nine dots is a heptagon.

This is one way of doing it.

This is a way of drawing a polygon with sixteen sides on a grid of sixteen dots.

On a grid of twenty-five dots, it is possible to draw a polygon with twenty-four sides.

You can draw other polygons with just as many sides on the grids.

● Are these polygons convex?

Drawing Regular Polygons in a circle

30

All regular polygons will fit exactly into a circle. This makes most of them easy to draw with a compass, a ruler and pencil and a protractor.

A reminder about angles.

A complete circle is 360°.

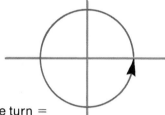

1 complete turn =
4 right angles = 360°

To draw a regular nonagon

1. With a compass, draw a circle with a **radius** of 2 inches.

2. A nonagon has nine sides, so you need to divide the circle into nine equal parts.

You can do this by dividing the angle at the center into nine equal parts. You need to divide 360° into nine equal angles.

$360 \div 9 = 40$

With a protractor and pencil, measure off and mark 40° nine times. You should finish where you started.

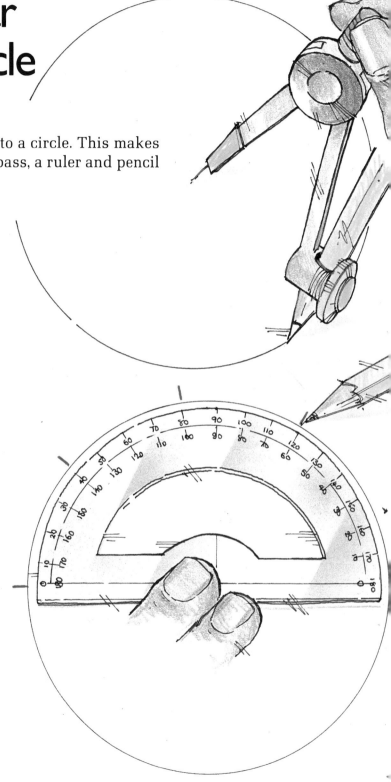

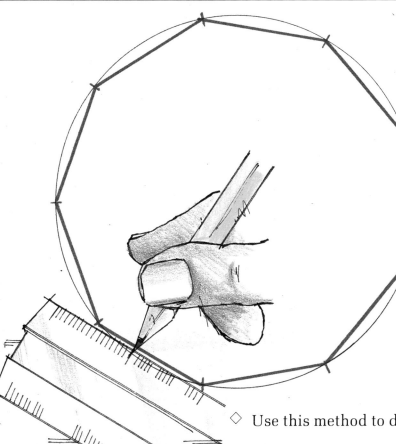

3. Use a ruler and the angle marks to mark off the **circumference** of the circle into nine equal sections.

4. Join the nine points to make a regular nonagon.

◇ Use this method to draw a regular pentagon of your own.

Checkpoints

a. Check with a ruler that each of the sides of your finished regular pentagon is the same length.

b. Check with a protractor that each of the angles of your regular pentagon is the same size.

If your angles vary by only 1 or 2 degrees, this is acceptable because it is difficult to measure and draw completely accurately.

> **If your pentagon has gone seriously wrong, follow the guidelines on page 32.**

● **1.** Why doesn't this method work very well when you use it to draw a regular heptagon?

Guidelines for drawing a regular pentagon

A pentagon has five sides, so the problem you need to solve is
$360 \div 5 = 72$

Make sure that you have measured 72° **each** time. Check with a
protractor.

Making sure

● **1.** If you want to draw a regular decagon, what problem do you
need to work out?

● **2.** How will you use the answer?

A POLYGON PATTERN

In the pattern below, a line has been drawn to join each **vertex** of
the nonagon from page 31 to every other vertex. **1** has been joined
to **3, 4, 5, 6, 7** and **8**. (**1** to **2** and **1** to **9** form edges of the nonagon
already.) **2** has been joined to **4, 5, 6, 7, 8** and **9** and so on.

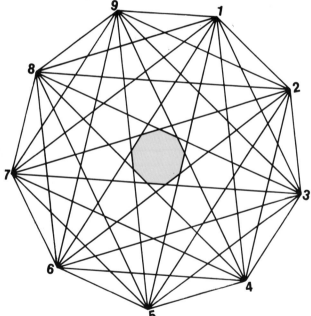

Look at the colored shape in the middle of the pattern. It is a
smaller regular nonagon.

● Experiment with your regular pentagon. Join all the vertices to
each other. What happens?

Tangram

A tangram is a set of shapes cut from a square. You can use it in many ways. It originated in China many years ago. You can buy tangram sets, but it is very easy to make your own. All you need is a 5 inch square of thick paper or thin cardboard, a pencil, ruler and scissors.

A set square is useful to help you to draw the parallel lines.

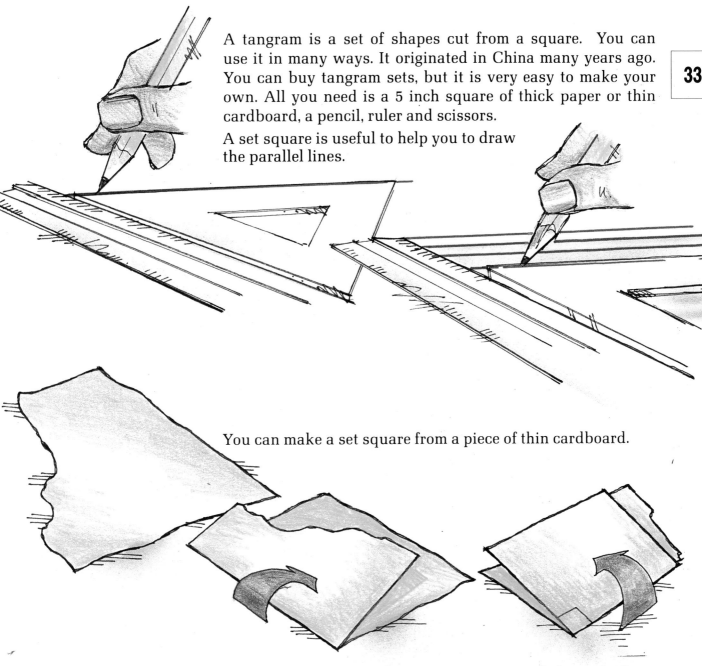

You can make a set square from a piece of thin cardboard.

Try to be accurate with your measuring, and draw the lines with a ruler.

To make a tangram set

◇ **1.** Draw a diagonal line across the square from the bottom left hand corner to the top right hand corner.

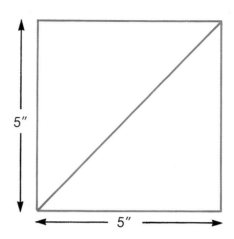

◇ **2.** Measure $2\frac{1}{2}$ inches along the bottom of the square and $2\frac{1}{2}$ inches up the right hand side. Draw a line **parallel** to the diagonal.

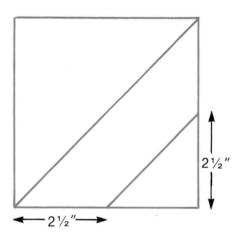

◇ **3.** Draw a diagonal from the top left hand corner to meet the line you drew in step 2.

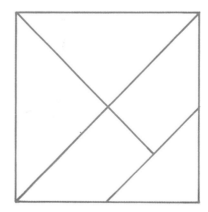

34

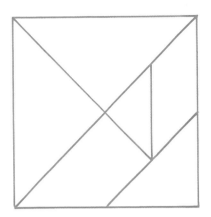

◇ **4.** Draw a **vertical** line from the point where the lines from steps 2 and 3 **intersect** until it meets the first diagonal.

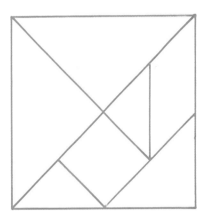

◇ **5.** Draw a line, parallel to the second diagonal, from the bottom halfway mark to the first diagonal.

● **6.** Carefully cut out your pieces. Color them if you want them to look more attractive. How many triangles do you have? What are the names of the other two pieces?

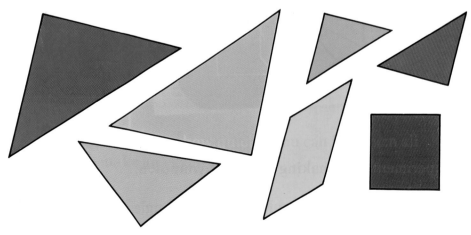

Interior Angles and Polygons

38

In these polygons a **vertex** has been marked with a cross and then joined by a **diagonal** to each of the other vertices, except the two adjacent ones.

● Why can't you draw a diagonal from a vertex to the one next to it?

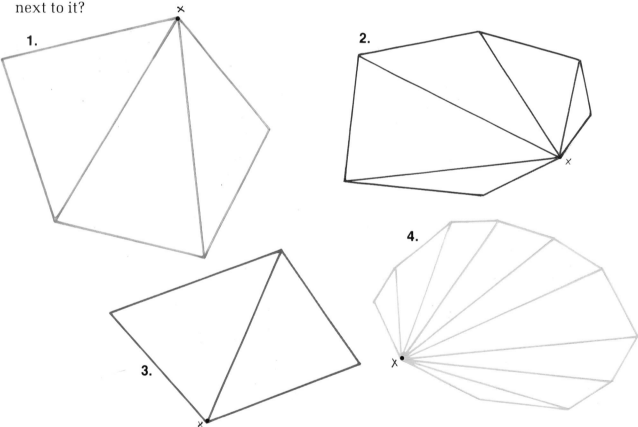

● **a.** What is the name of each of the polygons?

● **b.** What is the name of the shapes made by the diagonals.

Draw some convex polygons of your own. Mark one of the vertices and from it draw as many diagonals as you can.

● Look at your diagrams. For each one, count the number of sides and the number of triangles you have made inside it by drawing diagonals.

● What is the connection between the number of sides and the number of triangles?

For the diagrams on page 38 the results are:

Name of Shape	Number of Sides	Number of Triangles
1. Pentagon	5	3
2. Heptagon	7	5
3. Quadrilateral	4	2
4. Eleven-sided polygon	11	9

Answers to tangram puzzles

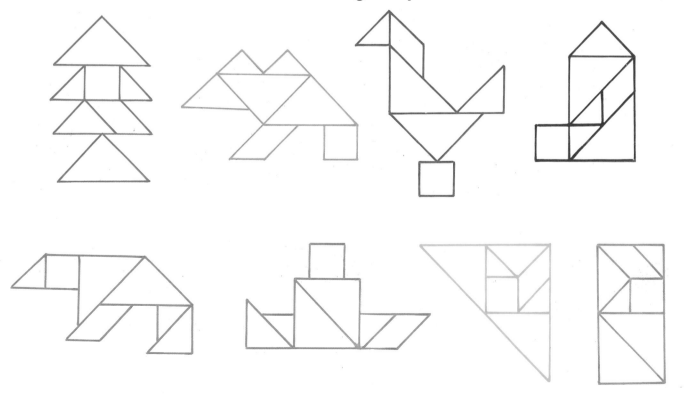

The connection between the number of sides and the number of triangles is that there are always **two fewer triangles than the number of sides**.

If you look at the **interior** angles of the polygon, you can see that the angles of the triangles join together to make them.

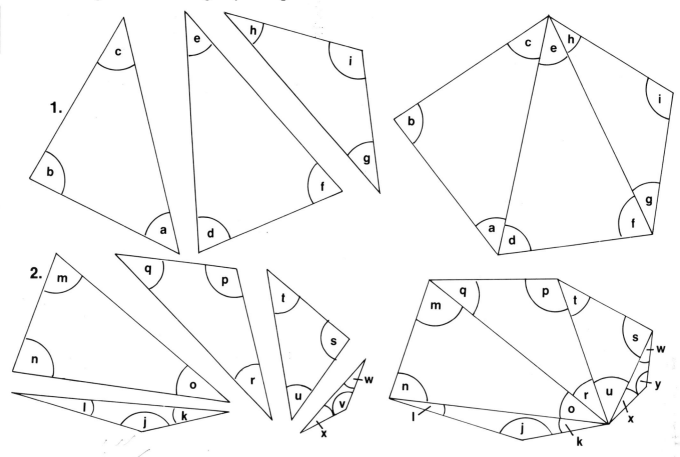

The sum of the angles of the triangles and the sum of the interior angles of the polygon are equal.

The angles of a triangle $= 180°$

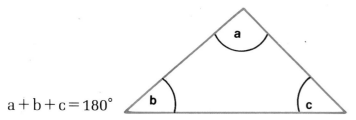

$a + b + c = 180°$

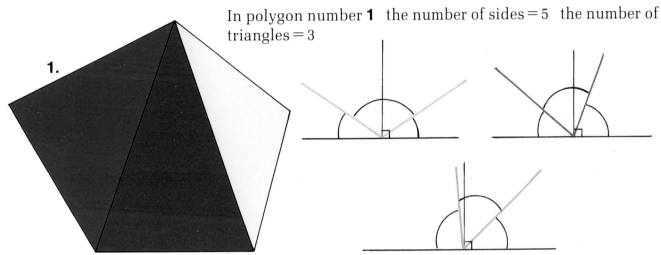

In polygon number **1** the number of sides = 5 the number of triangles = 3

The angles of each triangle will fit on a straight line. The sum of the angles of each triangle is 180°.

The sum of the interior angles of the pentagon
= 3 × 180° = 540°

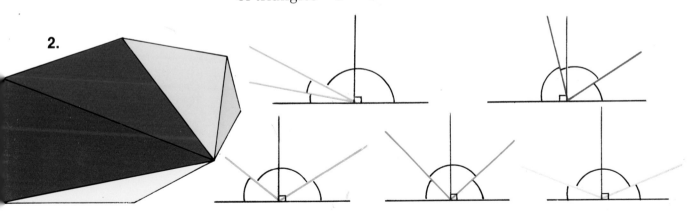

In polygon number **2** the number of sides = 7 the number of triangles = 5

The sum of the interior angles of the heptagon
= 5 × 180° = 900°

The sum of the interior angles of any polygon = (the number of sides of the polygon - 2) × 180°.

● Figure out the sum of the interior angles of polygons **3** and **4**.

● Use what you know about the sum of the interior angles of a polygon to calculate the size of the four angles **a** to **d** in the diagrams below. Do not try to measure them. You may use a calculator.

42

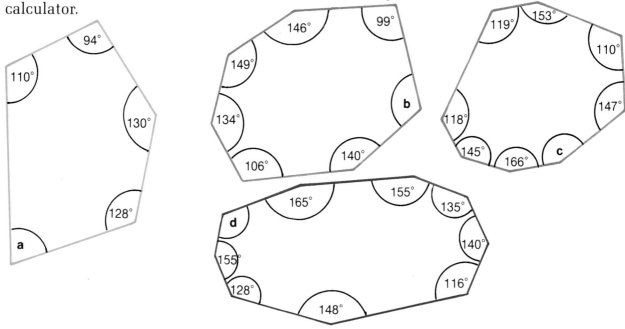

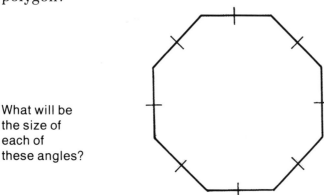

If you are stuck, the example on the next page will help.

Puzzle

Interior angles and regular polygons

The angles of a regular polygon are all equal. How can you figure out the size of each of the interior angles of any regular polygon?

What will be the size of each of these angles?

Working out the missing angle in a polygon

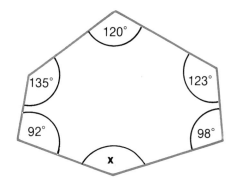

The polygon is a hexagon.
The sum of its interior angles $= 4 \times 180° = 720°$.
The sum of the five given angles $=$
$92° + 135° + 120° + 123° + 98° = 568°$.
Angle $\mathbf{x} = 720 - 568 = 152°$.

Answer to Easter tangram

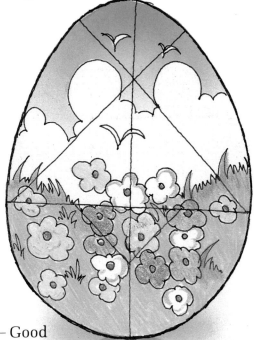

How did you rate?
Less then five minutes – Good
Less than two minutes – Excellent
Less than one minute – Are you sure you didn't cheat!

Calculating Interior Angles of Regular Polygons

44

Answer to puzzle on page 42

The polygon is an octagon.
The sum of the interior angles $= 6 \times 180° = 1,080°$.
There are 8 **equal** interior angles.
Each interior angle $= 1,080° \div 8 = 135°$.

To calculate the interior angles of a regular polygon, you find the sum of the angles [(the number of sides - 2) $\times$ 180°] and **divide the sum of the angles by the number of angles**.

Copy this table and fill in the gaps. Do not write in the book.

Regular Polygon	Sum of Interior Angles	Number of Angles	Size of Each Angle
	360°	4	90°
Pentagon		5	
Hexagon		6	120°
Heptagon	900°		
Octagon	1080°		
Nonagon		9	
Decagon	1440°		

Drawing Regular Polygons

Now that you can work out the size of the interior angles of any regular polygon you can draw any regular polygon to the size you need.

To draw an octagon with sides 2 inches long

1. Leave a space of about 6 inches, and with a ruler, draw a line **AB** 2 inches long.

2. Each interior angle of a regular octagon = 135° (see page 44). With a protractor, measure angles of 135° at each end of the line.

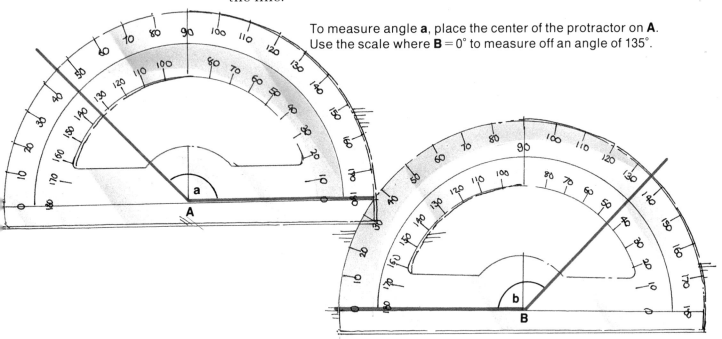

To measure angle **a**, place the center of the protractor on **A**. Use the scale where **B** = 0° to measure off an angle of 135°.

To measure angle **b**, place the center of the protractor on **B**. Use the scale where **A** = 0° to measure off an angle of 135°.

3. With a ruler, measure off 2 inches along each of the 135°
angle lines and draw sides **2** and **3**.

4. Place the protractor at the end of side 2. Measure off 135°
and draw side 4 (2 inches long).

5. Place the protractor at the end of side 3 and draw side 5.

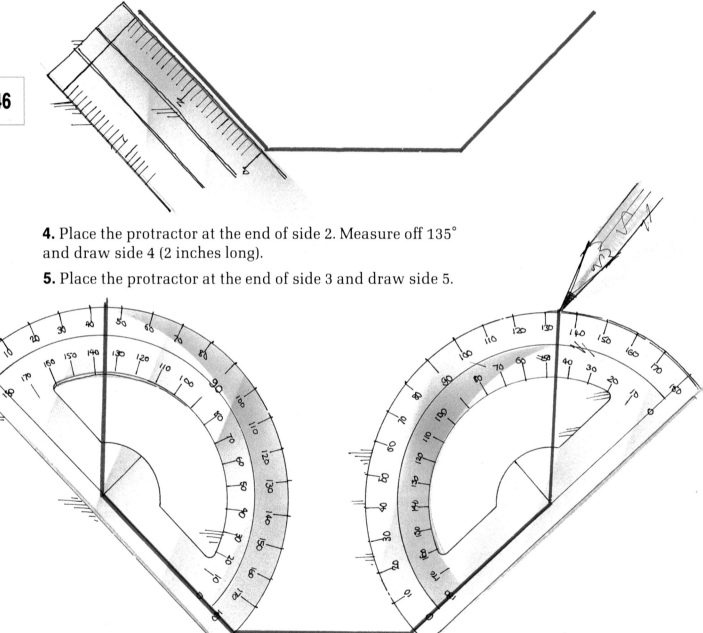

6. Use the protractor and ruler to draw sides 6 and 7.

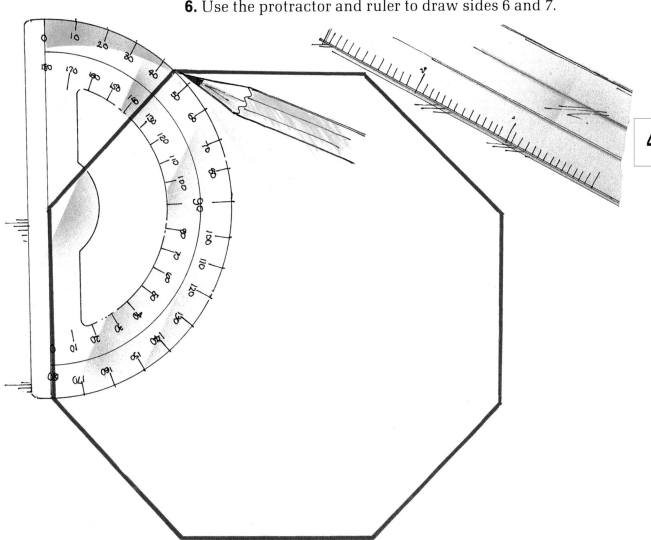

7. If you have measured accurately, you will have a gap of 2 inches, which you join up to draw side 8.

Use this method to draw a regular dodecagon with sides $\frac{1}{2}''$ long. You will need to cut up your dodecagon later, so use scrap paper. It is important that you make your dodecagon as accurate as possible.

The ancient Babylonians lived about 4,000 years ago in what today is Iraq. It was probably they who first had the idea of dividing a complete circle into 360 parts, what we now call degrees. They divided the year into 360 days and counted in sixties instead of tens like we do. 360 is a good number to choose for angles in a complete circle. Because 360 has many **factors**, it is easy to divide a circle into equal parts and to draw most regular polygons.

48

Each of the regular polygons in the table on page 44 has a number of angles that divides exactly into 180 or 360, so that the size of each angle is a whole number. This does not always happen. This is the reason that it is difficult to draw a regular heptagon.

Each angle of a regular heptagon =
[(number of sides - 2) × 180] ÷ 7 =
[(7 - 2) × 180] ÷ 7 =
(5 × 180) ÷ 7 =
900 ÷ 7 = 128.58°
(to 2 decimal places)

The nearest you can measure with a protractor is $128\frac{1}{2}°$.
The same thing happens if you try to measure the angle at the center of a circle to draw a regular heptagon inside it.
360° ÷ 7 = 51.43° (to 2 decimal places)

● Which other regular polygons, up to twenty sides, can you not draw perfectly accurately with a protractor?

All Square

Your regular dodecagon, with $\frac{1}{2}''$ sides, should be **congruent** with this one.

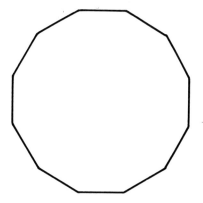

Draw in these four **diagonals**.

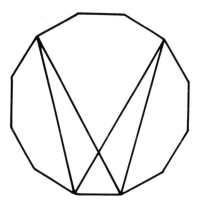

- Cut your dodecagon into six pieces. What are the names of these pieces?

- Can you rearrange the pieces to form a square?

Warning: it will only work if your drawing and cutting is accurate.

Making a Flexihexi

You need a strip of thin cardboard at least 9 inches long and 2 inches wide, scissors, a protractor and some paper glue. The cardboard needs to be plain and the same color on both sides.

1. Construct ten equilateral triangles with $1\frac{1}{2}$ inch sides as shown in the diagram below. You can use the protractor method – an equilateral triangle is a regular polygon – or you can use a compass if you find it easier. Measure and draw as accurately as you can. Label triangles as shown.

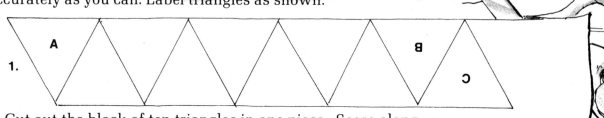

2. Cut out the block of ten triangles in one piece. Score along the lines so that they fold easily. Bend each line, in turn, forward and backward.

Mark a red line.

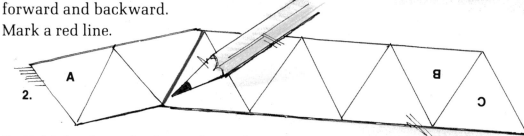

3. Fold backward along the red line to make this shape. The back of the cardboard is now showing in the bottom six triangles.

Mark a green line as shown.

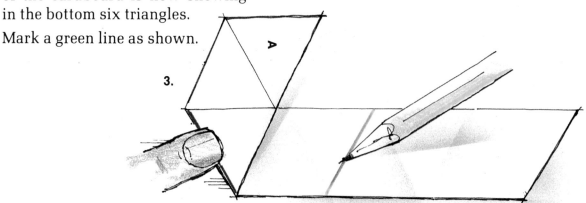

4. Rotate the card so that the red line is at the bottom. Fold the top of the shape backward at the green line so that it goes down behind triangle **A** like this.

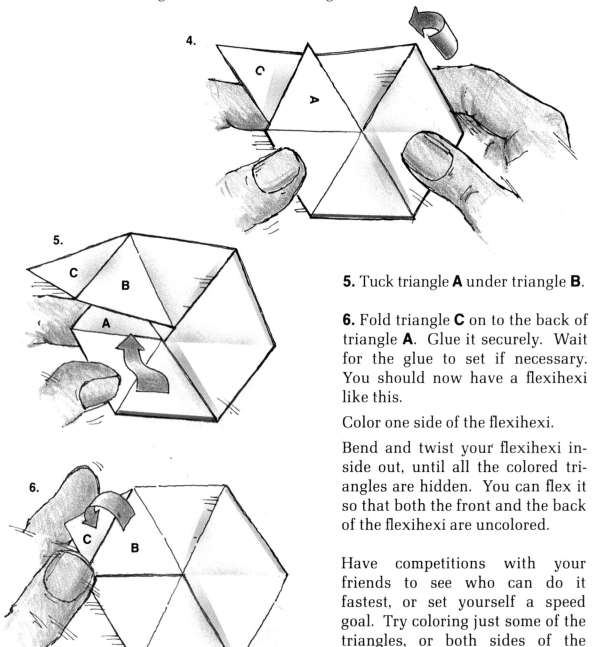

5. Tuck triangle **A** under triangle **B**.

6. Fold triangle **C** on to the back of triangle **A**. Glue it securely. Wait for the glue to set if necessary. You should now have a flexihexi like this.

Color one side of the flexihexi.

Bend and twist your flexihexi inside out, until all the colored triangles are hidden. You can flex it so that both the front and the back of the flexihexi are uncolored.

Have competitions with your friends to see who can do it fastest, or set yourself a speed goal. Try coloring just some of the triangles, or both sides of the flexihexi, and see what happens.

Simple Stars for Christmas

This is an easy way of making stars for Christmas decorations. Practice with scrap paper first and use pretty paper or thin cardboard for your final efforts.

Six and twelve pointed stars

1. Fold a rectangle of paper in half.

2. Fold the bottom left hand corner up toward the top of the paper at an angle of 60°. Check with a protractor.

3. Fold the top left hand corner over toward the first fold at 60°. If you have measured accurately, the folds and edges will meet exactly.

4. Fold the bottom fold to meet the top fold.

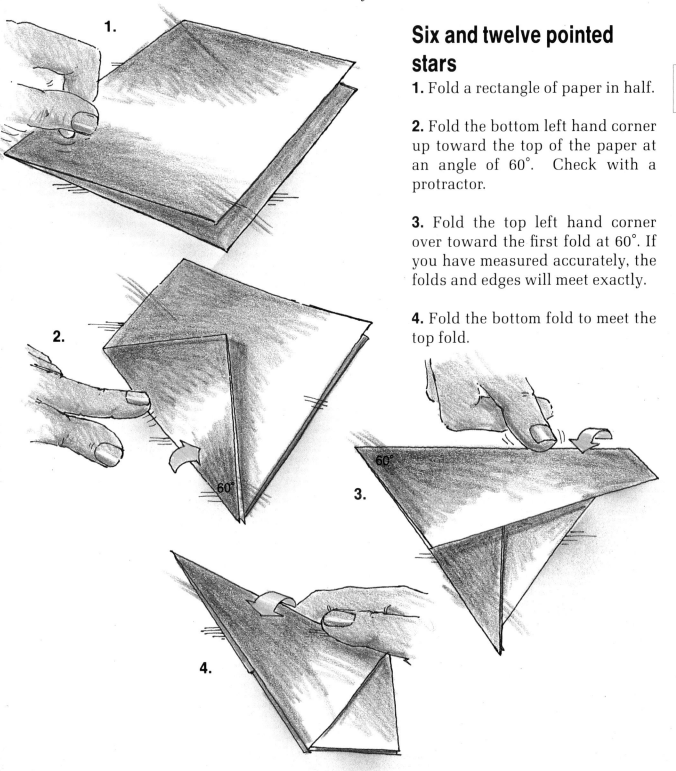

5. Cut off a triangle from the pointed end.

6. Unfold the triangle to reveal a six-pointed star. Fold all the long folds, which go across the points of the star, one way up and all the short folds the other way up. This will make the star look three-dimensional.

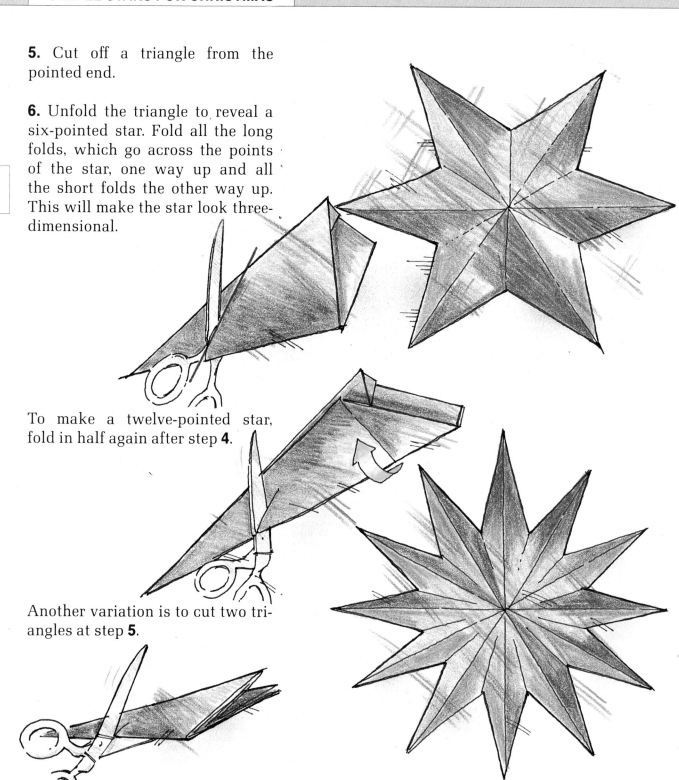

To make a twelve-pointed star, fold in half again after step **4**.

Another variation is to cut two triangles at step **5**.

◇ Try it and see what happens.

Five and ten pointed stars

1. Fold a piece of paper in half as before.

Fold the bottom left hand corner up to the middle of the top edge of the paper.

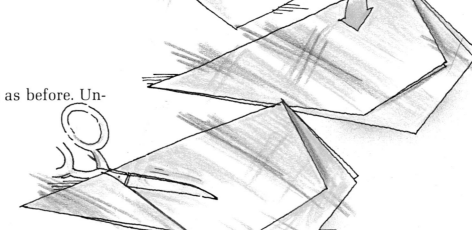

2. Fold the top left hand corner over the edge **AB**.

3. Fold along the line **CD**.

4. Cut off a triangle as before. Unfold your star.

- You cannot make alternate folds for a three-dimensional look on a **pentangle**. Why not?

- How can you make a ten-pointed star?

- How can you make a ten-pointed star with a pentangle cut out of the middle?

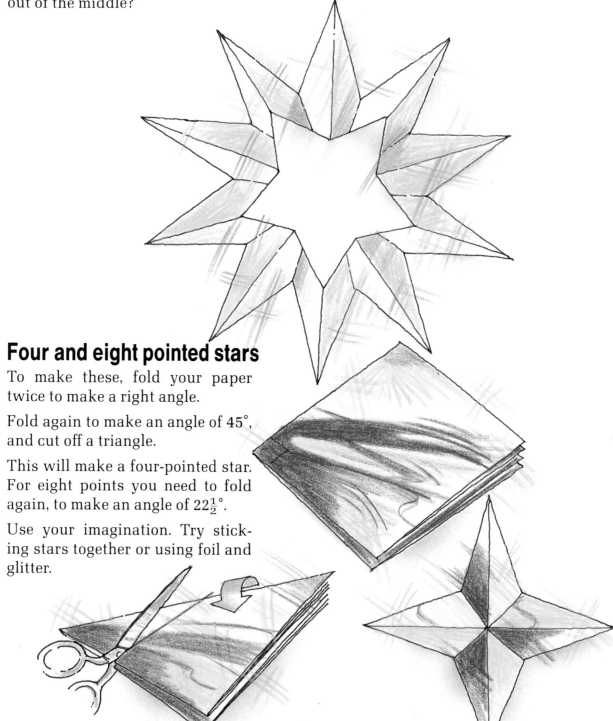

Four and eight pointed stars

To make these, fold your paper twice to make a right angle.

Fold again to make an angle of 45°, and cut off a triangle.

This will make a four-pointed star. For eight points you need to fold again, to make an angle of $22\frac{1}{2}°$.

Use your imagination. Try sticking stars together or using foil and glitter.

Twist and Shake

You need plenty of scrap paper and some paper glue. Cut four long strips: pieces about 2 inches wide and at least 12 inches long. Color one side of each strip.

1. Take one of the strips and glue the ends together to make a loop.

● **a.** Can you say whether the colored side of the strip is the inside or the outside of the loop?

● **b.** Cut along the center of the strip. What do you get?

2. Take a second strip. Twist it once and then glue the ends together to make a loop. This is called a Moebius strip, after the nineteenth century German mathematician who first investigated it.

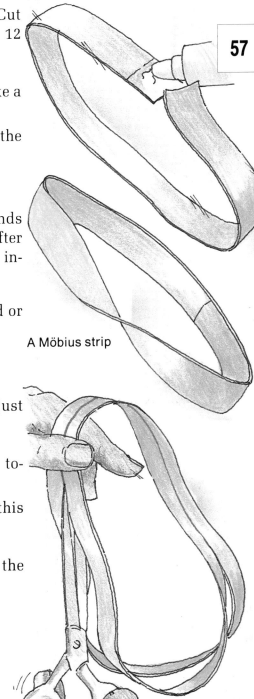

A Möbius strip

● **a.** Can you say whether the inside of the loop is colored or not?

b) Draw a line along the middle of the inside of the loop.

● What happens?

c. Cut the strip along the center line that you have just drawn. What do you get?

3. Take a third strip. Twist it twice and stick the ends together to make a loop.

● What do you get if you cut along the center of the strip this time?

● **4.** What do you think you will get when you cut along the center of a loop with three twists?

◇ Try it and see if you are right.

Knot a Regular Pentagon

58

You need a rectangular strip of paper about 1 inch wide and 12 inches long.

Tie it in an ordinary knot, pull it tight and flatten it carefully.

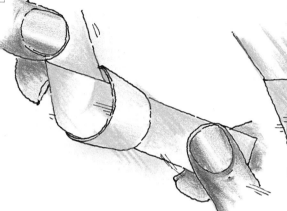

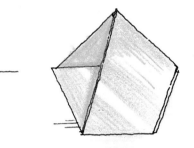

Cut off the ends and you have a regular pentagon.

Match This

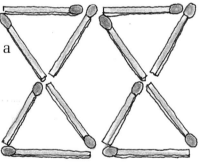

● Move four matches to make a regular hexagon.

Three Into One

Draw three regular hexagons on scrap paper. Cut out one whole. Cut up the second one into six equilateral triangles. Cut up the third into the parts shown below.

● Use all the pieces of the three hexagons to make one large regular hexagon.

Glossary

adjacent next to.

bisect to cut into two halves. It usually refers to cutting a line or angle into two halves.

circumference the boundary line that encloses a circle or the distance around the edge of a circle.

concentric having the same center. It usually refers to a set of circles which all have the same center. The ripples from a stone thrown into a pond form concentric circles.

congruent two shapes are congruent when they are the same size and shape; one will fit exactly on top of the other.

convex in a convex polygon, it is impossible to draw a line that joins two points on its edges and also passes outside the polygon.

decagon a polygon with ten sides.

diagonal a line joining two vertices of a polygon, where the vertices are not adjacent to each other.

diameter a line passing through the center of a circle from one point on the circumference to another point on the circumference.

dodecagon a polygon with twelve sides.

ellipse a regular closed curve formed by the path of a point that moves so the sum of its distance from two points is always the same.

heptagon a polygon with seven sides.

hexagon a polygon with six sides.

intersect a line intersects with another when it cuts across it.

nonagon a polygon with nine sides.

octagon a polygon with eight sides.

parallel parallel lines will never intersect; they always remain the same distance apart. Railway tracks are made from pairs of parallel lines.

60

parallelogram a quadrilateral with two pairs of parallel lines.

pentagon a polygon with five sides.

pentagram or pentangle a star shape with five points.

polygon a closed shape with straight sides.

quadrilateral a polygon with four sides.

radius the distance from the center of a circle to the circumference.

right angle an angle of 90°; a quarter of a turn.

solid a three-dimensional object.

sphere a perfectly regular ball; a solid in which every point on the surface is at the same distance from the center.

trapezoid a quadrilateral with one pair of parallel lines.

vertex the point where two edges of a polygon meet. The plural of vertex is vertices.

vertical upright. A plumb line hangs vertically.

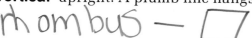

Answers

Page 8
To draw the top of a can, see page11.

Page 9
These are the closed shapes.

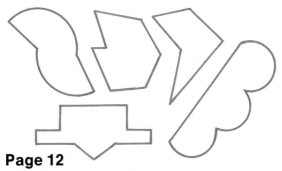

Page 12
The shape is an ellipse.

Page 17
See page 18.

Page 18
1. A triangle is the name of the polygon with the fewest possible sides.
2. A convex polygon with very many small sides begins to look like a curved shape.
For answers to five dots puzzle, see page 21.

Page 19
For answers to grid, see page 26.

Page 20
For answers to Making polygons, see page 24.

Page 21
For answers to triangles and five dots, see page 28.

Page 23

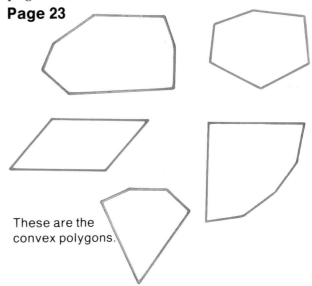

These are the convex polygons.

It is not possible to draw a triangle which is not convex. All triangles are convex.

Page 25
See page 26.

62

Page 26
See page 28.
Page 27
See page 29.
Page 28

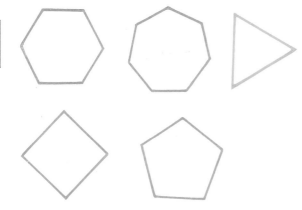

Page 29
The polygons are not convex.
Page 31
See page 48.
Page 32
1. The problem you would need to work out for a regular decagon is $360 \div 10 = 36$.
2. With a protractor and pencil, measure and mark ten angles of $36°$ at the center of a circle. Use a ruler, positioned on the center of the circle and each of the $36°$ marks in turn, to mark off ten equally spaced sections on the circumference. Join up these marks.
Page 32
You get a pentagon in the middle. You can draw diagonals in the new pentagon, if it is big enough, and you will get another smaller pentagon. Draw a large pentagon and see how many times you can make a pentagon inside it. To get good results, your must draw your first pentagon accurately.

Page 35
There are five triangles, a square and a parallelogram.
Page 36
See page 39.
Page 37
See page 43.
Page 38
Adjacent vertices form the sides of the polygon.
a) 1. pentagon **2.** heptagon **3.** quadrilateral **4.** no special; name – eleven-sided polygon.
b) the diagonals make triangles.
Page 39
See page 40.
Page 41
The sum of the interior angles of polygon 3 is $1,620°$ ($180° \times 9$).
The sum of the interior angles of polygon 4 is $360°$ ($180° \times 2$).
Page 42
Angle **a)** is one of the angles of a pentagon. The sum of the interior angles of a pentagon $= 540°$ ($180° \times 3$). The rest of the angles of the pentagon total $462°$. Therefore angle **a)** is $540° - 462° = 78°$.
Angle **b)** $= 900° - 774° = 126°$
Angle **c)** $= 1,080° - 958° = 122°$
Angle **d)** $= 1,260° - 1,142° = 118°$

Regular Polygon	Sum of Interior Angles	Number of Angles	Size of Each Angle
Square	360°	4	90°
Pentagon	540°	5	108°
Hexagon	720°	6	120°
Heptagon	900°	7	128.6°
Octagon	1080°	8	135°
Nonagon	1260°	9	140°
Decagon	1440°	10	144°

Page 42
Puzzle see page 44.

Page 48
11-sided, 13-sided, 14-sided, 17-sided and 19-sided.

Page 49
3 triangles and 3 pentagons.

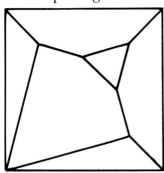

Page 54
You get a star with a star cut out in the middle.

Page 56
You cannot make alternate folds because 5 is an odd number.

You make a ten-pointed star by folding in half again after step 3.

You make a ten-pointed star with a pentangle cut out by cutting off a small triangle after step 3 and before putting in the extra fold for a ten-pointed star.

Page 57
1. a) Yes **b)** two separate loops
2. a) No **b)** the line continues inside and outside the loop **c)** one loop with two twists
3. Two inter-linked loops, each of which has one twist
4.

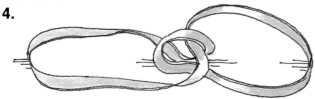

Page 58

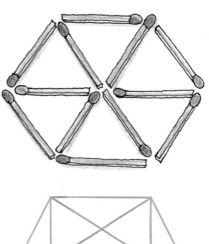

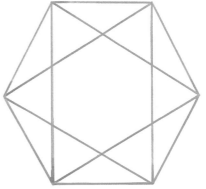

Index